POSITIVE THOUGHTS LEAD TO SUCCESS

A QUOTE BOOK

NEHA GUPTA

Made with ♥ on the Notion Press Platform
www.notionpress.com

“”

Contents

Contents

Contents

Contents

Contents

About The Author

Neha Gupta is a driven individual who loves to help, motivate, and encourage young people. She is all about growth and development and wishes to make the world a better place. She has also written a fictional novel, *What it feels like growing up as a girl?* which has become a heart-touching novel for her readers. She has received numerous prestigious awards for her literary contributions over the years. She believes in herself and enjoys seizing new opportunities.

Acknowledgements

I would like to express my deepest gratitude to all those who have supported me throughout the journey of writing this book, "Positive Thoughts Lead to Success." Their unwavering belief in my abilities and their continuous encouragement have been instrumental in bringing this project to fruition.

First and foremost, I would like to thank my family for their endless love, understanding, and patience. Their support has been my rock, providing me with the strength and motivation to pursue my passion for writing and personal development.

I am incredibly grateful to my editor, whose expertise and guidance have been invaluable in shaping this book. Their insightful feedback and meticulous attention to detail have elevated the quality of the content, making it a better and more impactful read.

I would also like to extend my appreciation to the team at my publisher for their dedication and professionalism in bringing this book to the world. Their commitment to excellence and belief in the importance of spreading positive messages have been instrumental in making this project a reality.

To my friends and colleagues who have cheered me on and provided valuable insights along the way, thank you for being a source of inspiration and for sharing your wisdom and experiences. Your presence in my life has enriched me both personally and professionally.

Finally, I want to express my heartfelt gratitude to the readers of this book. Your openness to new ideas and your willingness to embark on a journey of personal growth and success are what make writing this book so fulfilling. I hope that the pages you hold in your hands will empower you to cultivate a positive mindset and unlock the success you deserve.

Thank you, each and every one of you, for being a part of this incredible journey. May your lives be filled with positivity, abundance, and endless success.

With gratitude,

Neha Gupta

Preface

Dear Reader,

Welcome to "Positive Thoughts Lead to Success," a book dedicated to exploring the power of positive thinking and its profound impact on achieving success in all areas of life. In these pages, I aim to enlighten and inspire you, offering insights, strategies, and real-life examples that will empower you to transform your mindset and unlock your full potential.

I firmly believe that our thoughts shape our reality. When we cultivate a positive mindset, we invite abundance, happiness, and success into our lives. By harnessing the immense power of our thoughts, we can overcome obstacles, navigate challenges, and create a fulfilling life that aligns with our dreams and aspirations.

Through extensive research, personal experiences, and interactions with successful individuals, I have witnessed the transformative effects of positive thinking firsthand. The journey towards success begins within ourselves, as we learn to harness the power of our thoughts and beliefs. This book will guide you on that transformative journey, providing practical tools and techniques to cultivate a positive mindset and embrace the opportunities that come your way.

As you embark on this exploration, remember that positive thinking is not about ignoring reality or suppressing negative emotions. Rather, it is a conscious choice to focus on the bright side of life, to reframe challenges as opportunities, and to maintain an optimistic outlook even in the face of adversity. It is a mindset that enables us to tap into our inherent strengths and create the life we desire.

I encourage you to approach this book with an open mind and a willingness to embrace change. Reflect on the concepts and exercises provided, and apply them to your daily life. With commitment, practice, and persistence, you will witness the remarkable impact positive thoughts can have on your personal growth, relationships, career, and overall well-being.

I am thrilled to be your guide on this transformative journey, and I am confident that the principles shared within these pages will empower you to unlock the success you deserve. Together, let us embark on a path of positive thinking, self-discovery, and limitless possibilities.

Wishing you an abundance of positivity and success,

Neha Gupta

1

*"Be the best version of yourself!
Don't let others define you."*

2

"This is your life, not someone else's.
Live your life the way you want to."

"Believe in yourself, not the words of others,
If you wish to improve your life."

4

"Don't be in pursuit of love.
Go after your dreams.
Love will find its way to you."

"If you are walking the journey all by yourself,
Stay calm.
Everyone who has achieved success,
Has been in this spot."

"Don't wish to change others, change yourself,
To reach the goals you have set for yourself."

*"Be positive even in a negative situation,
Don't let pessimism win over your thoughts."*

*"If you consider life to be tough,
Life would become more challenging.
Life would become easier,
If you reckon it would be."*

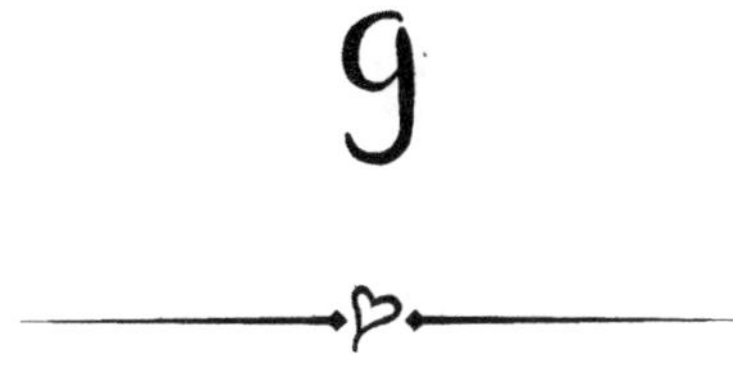

"Successful people don't wait for the ideal moment. They transform the toughest moments into the best moments."

10

*"Instead of wishing other people to stumble,
Give it your all to do something that will make
you stand out."*

"Your success hinges on your behaviour. Alter your habits before you make plans for the future."

12

"Falling in love with others could shatter you. Show yourself some love, and you will be rewarded."

*"Falling in love with others could break you,
Falling in love with yourself would make you."*

14

"If you stay focused on your destined path, success will be yours."

"Make sure your opinion is what matters most. The opinion of others takes a back seat."

*"Don't let yourself get sidetracked.
It was the main roadblock to your future."*

"Don't let your feeling of solitude keep you from achieving greatness.
Aching loneliness can be the price you pay for getting what you want."

"Make sure the people you associate with are the right ones.
Don't surround yourself with those who have a negative outlook."

*"Nobody took the reins when it came to your dreams.
Analyze yourself and strive for your dreams on your own."*

20

"Refrain from evaluating yourself from someone else's point of view.
Compare and contrast your current self to who you were before."

21

"Don't let yourself be disheartened if you don't succeed the first time.
Life offers multiple opportunities to achieve success instead of failure."

"Just dreaming about your dream job won't get you there.
Executing plans effectively is essential for achieving success."

23

"Don't let anything stand in your way. Conquer all the obstacles before they conquer you."

24

"It's a cinch to get what you want.
Just put your trust in your own talents."

25

*"Reflect on your failures.
Success will be yours one day."*

26

*"Put in the effort without making a fuss.
Let your accomplishments speak for themselves."*

27

"Try to avoid labour that is too strenuous. Exercise your intelligence to reach your objectives effectively."

28

"Don't be scared of what you might have to give up. Keep your eye on what you can acquire."

29

"Don't let life's hardships bring you down,
Stay strong and act like everything's okay.
Mighty walls might quake,
But they never succumb to defeat."

"The ones with strength don't have an easy journey. They light the way out of the darkness."

31

"Everyone experiences hardships in life. Learning and overcoming difficult situations are the facts of life."

32

"Distractions will always pop up,
When you make a move toward your goal.
But by shrugging off those distractions,
you can achieve success."

33

"Accomplishments can't be achieved in the blink of an eye.

After a couple of years of hard work, you make it to the top of the mountain."

"Put yourself first in matters of the heart. It's not being selfish, it's being loving towards yourself."

"Struggles won't come to an end.
But the challenging phases of your life,
Can be the keystone to gaining success."

"If you are unable to obtain what you are aiming for,
It's certain that you will receive what you deserve."

37

"You won't have enough time to experience everything,
Let the wisdom of others guide you to success."

"Those who always look for your flaws,
Don't even let their shadow cross your path."

39

"If others don't approve of what you're up to,
Don't let their viewpoint sway your choice."

*"Be generous and kindhearted,
This will give you an edge over everyone else."*

"Don't be downcast when things don't turn out the way you wanted.

Though failure can seem daunting, it's only a momentary setback."

"Losing something doesn't have to mean you have failed;
Not trying to get what you need will be seen as a failure."

"The person gazing back at you in the mirror is your greatest ally."

"Give yourself a break if you're feeling down.
Take time to be with yourself and appreciate your worth.
Revitalize and restart from scratch."

"Success doesn't always equate to having millions in your pocket.
But also your satisfaction, serenity, and welfare."

"The pathway to the destination is never-ending,
It will stay with you until your last breath.
Be sure to be better than you were the day before,
To move one step nearer to your ambitions."

"If finishing the task in a single day is out of the question,
Split it up into smaller tasks and get it done.
But don't ever give up on it or abandon it midway."

48

"You will receive a barrage of pebbles,
When you pursue your dreams.
But everyone will greet you warmly,
When your pocket contains billions of dollars."

"Don't put energy into trying to prove yourself to others.
Spend some time reading to broaden your learning."

*"The chattering of others will cease,
Once you start bringing your accomplishments to light.
"*

"Don't attempt to imitate someone else's journey!
Rather build yourself an extraordinary persona,
And you will be looked up to as a role model by others.
Your worth will be cherished even after you have left this world."

“”

"Refrain from taking revenge!
Rather drive forward with fresh intensity.
Put forth more effort to refine your skills,
And let the world listen to the noise of your success."

"Don't expect success to be handed to you on a silver platter.
It won't ever happen!
Step up and take charge of yourself,
And smash all the records to accomplish your goals."

55

"Don't rely solely on destiny,
Because fate doesn't always work out.
However, effort does."

"An ordinary person will be found,
In the midst of their kind.
While those who are special,
Will eventually find,
The pinnacle of accomplishment by themselves."

57

"If you never take a chance in life,
You will never grow.
Taking risks is the key to success,
Not a sign of failure."

"There is an individual who has the potential to revolutionize your life.
Just glance at your reflection in the mirror."

"Showing off is a symptom of a weak character. The actions of strong people speak louder than words."

"Until you make a decision, no one can alter your fate."

"Wrap up your explanations to others,
And be mindful of your inner guidance."

62

"If the skies are cloudy today,
Hope for better weather tomorrow."

63

"Traditional board games are old,
Mind games are the new way of life."

*"Reality is often hidden behind a facade.
It could be different than what you think."*

65

"Patience and hard work will give you something unique in the end,
But you need to be composed."

"Always be proud of who you are!
Don't let others dictate who you should be."

"The failures have thousands of reasons to not try. People who have succeeded have just one reason to keep striving."

"Never be ashamed to be the real you,
Stay true to your inner-self."

"Trust can either be the cornerstone of our success or the cause of our downfall."

"Giving up is easy, but sticking to the end is hard.
The ease of life yields nothing,
But the difficulty of life yields returns."

"If somebody says to you, "You can't do it." Refrain from responding with words. Make an impact with your results."

72

"Let the haters be!
Don't let them bring you down.
Let yourself go ahead with who you are."

"Spread positivity, and it will come back to you."

*"Don't try to fit in with the crowd.
Aim for success and people will follow."*

"Look inside yourself to recognize your strengths, And ensure that your objectives match up with your abilities."

76

"Don't be afraid to be judged by others,
But don't forget what you possess,
Is self-belief, self-confidence, and self- love."

*"The way we view the future right now,
We will construct our future in the same manner."*

78

"Life is more than just regretting failures.
Begin each day with a fresh start in life."

79

"When people start to acknowledge you,
With your own name instead of your father's ,
Enjoy the success you have achieved."

"Act towards others the same way you would like to be treated."

"When someone believes that you are not on their level,

Show them that you're not in the same league,

Rather a rank above."

*"Don't ever say that money doesn't matter.
In the end, money is all that really matters."*

"Make your goodwill so strong,
That no one dares to reject you."

"Sometimes, we should take the time to consider other possibilities.
The second option might be more advantageous than the first one."

*"The rewards of hard work are always worth it.
If not too early, then definitely too late."*

"Some people win hearts with words.
Some people win hearts through action.
Some people win hearts by silence.
Make a choice for yourself."

*"Silence can convey a multitude of messages.
It's necessary to read them with your eyes."*

"The best way to prove yourself,
don't prove yourself."

*"Ordinary people follow ordinary norms,
While exceptional people create their own
norms."*

*"Most breakable peoples are the ones,
Who make the most out of their life."*

91

*"If people make you crumble,
Refrain from giving them attention.
Because people make you fall,
When they can't muster the power to be with you."*

"Toxic people will remain toxic.
Neither they will make you;
Nor they will destroy you.
They will just take the advantage of you."

*"If you remain patient in your darkest hours.
Your fantasy life is almost within reach."*

"Experiencing exhaustion in the darkness.
Start off the morning with a clean slate
would make your journey a fruitful one."

"When you push yourself tirelessly towards attaining your goals, the universe rewards you for your efforts."

"A failure's demise is concentrating on the losses. Successful people never lose sight of their accomplishments."

"Taking action towards your goal is the key to unlocking the door."

98

"In the garden of your mind, choose to cultivate flowers of positivity. Their fragrance will attract success."

"Your thoughts are the architects of your destiny. Create a base of optimism, and achievement will be the crowning glory."

Author's Note

Dear Reader,

Thank you for joining me on this transformative journey of exploring the power of positive thoughts in achieving success. As we come to the end of this book, I would like to leave you with some final thoughts and resources to support you on your continued path to success.

Stay Committed: Remember that cultivating a positive mindset is an ongoing practice. Stay committed to nurturing positive thoughts and beliefs, even in the face of challenges. Embrace setbacks as opportunities for growth and keep moving forward.

Take Action: Positive thoughts alone are not enough. Take inspired action towards your goals. Set clear intentions, create action plans, and take consistent steps forward. Believe in yourself and your ability to achieve what you desire.

Surround Yourself with Positivity: Surround yourself with positive influences. Seek out supportive friends, mentors, and communities that uplift and inspire you. Engage in activities that bring you joy and nourish your spirit.

Gratitude: Cultivate an attitude of gratitude. Regularly express appreciation for the blessings in your life. Gratitude opens your heart and attracts more positive experiences.

Personal Development: Continue your journey of personal growth and development. Invest in yourself by reading books, attending seminars, and seeking knowledge that expands your horizons and deepens your understanding of success.

Resources: In addition to this book, there are numerous resources available to support you on your path to success. Explore books, podcasts, online courses, and workshops that align with your goals and interests. Allow these resources to expand your knowledge and inspire new insights.

Stay Positive: Remember that positivity is a choice. Even during challenging times, maintain a positive outlook. Embrace the lessons, grow from experiences, and believe in your ability to overcome any obstacles that come your way.

Share Your Story: As you experience success in your own life, share your journey with others. Inspire and uplift those around you. Your story has the power to ignite positive change in the lives of others.

Remember, success is a personal and unique journey. Embrace your individual path and celebrate your accomplishments, no matter how big or small. Believe in yourself and the limitless possibilities that await you.

Once again, I want to express my deepest gratitude for being a part of this transformative experience. It has been an honor to guide you on this journey, and I wish you abundant success, joy, and fulfillment in all your endeavors.

With heartfelt wishes for your continued success,

Neha Gupta

Printed by Libri Plureos GmbH in Hamburg,
Germany

9 798890 660633